From the Molly Learns Series

Molly Learns 10 Facts About Abraham Lincoln

By
Marla Harms Judge
and Molly the History Dog

In this photo, I pose with a wax statue of young Abraham Lincoln in nature. We are at the Abraham Lincoln Presidential Museum.

Copyright © 2022 Marla Harms Judge.
All rights reserved.

Book design by Madeline Littleton

ISBN Paperback 978-1-958533-06-2
ISBN Hardcover 978-1-958533-07-9

Library of Congress Control Number: 2022917676

Please write to us at: Mollythehistorydog@gmail.com
Visit: mollythehistorydog.com

Crippled Beagle Publishing, Knoxville, TN, USA
crippledbeaglepublishing.com

"All I have learned,
I learned
from books."
President Abraham
Lincoln

Hi! My name is Molly.
I am a dalmatian dog.
I am white with black spots.
Have you ever seen
a dalmatian?

Dalmatians are STARS in a couple of movies. Maybe you have seen one of these movies.

A hat like the one Abraham Lincoln wore looks stylish with my black spots.

My human family and I like to travel and learn about famous people and places.
I have lots of fun!

Today I want to tell you 10 facts I learned about a famous American. He was the 16th President of the United States.
He was tall and had a beard.
Can you guess who he was?

That's right. Abraham Lincoln!

FEBRUARY 1809

Sunday	Monday	Tuesday	Wednesday	Thursday	Friday	Saturday
			1	2	3	4
5	6	7	8	9	10	11
12	13	14	15	16	17	18
19	20	21	22	23	24	25
26	27	28				

One of the first facts I learned is that Abraham Lincoln was born on the cold morning of February 12, 1809, in Kentucky. That was a long time ago!
His parents were Thomas and Nancy Lincoln. He had a big sister named Sarah.

This log cabin is similar to Abraham Lincoln's birthplace.

His family lived in a log cabin. It did not have electricity. They did not have lights or a furnace. They burned wood in a fireplace to heat the cabin and cook meals.
Do you think you would like to cook on a fireplace? What would you cook?

There are many steps at the Abraham Lincoln Birthplace National Historic Park.

You can visit the place where he was born in Kentucky. There is a reconstructed cabin inside the building at the Abraham Lincoln Birthplace National Historic Park.

Young Abraham Lincoln reads while his dog snoozes. I would like to snooze by that fire. The photo of this scene was taken at the Abraham Lincoln Presidential Museum in Springfield, Illinois

Lincoln grew up on his family's farm. He worked hard to help his father. Because he was needed on the farm, young Abraham Lincoln had to miss school. Still, he read every chance he got.

Abraham Lincoln loved to read and learn. He often lay in front of the fireplace in the cabin at night to read by the firelight. When he was a boy, schools were unlike schools we have now. Students of all ages sat on long benches, and they all talked at the same time! They were called BLAB schools. I bet they were noisy!

I pose on a wooden bench in the schoolhouse at New Salem in Petersburg, Illinois. The school house at Lincoln's New Salem State Historic Site has been reconstructed..

When he was a young man, Lincoln lived in a place called New Salem, which was a nice small village where people lived in log houses. I visited New Salem. The village is rebuilt to look like it did when Lincoln lived there. My stroll through the area felt like walking back in time!

I pose with a living history interpreter.

People there called *living history interpreters* dress like the people did when Abraham lived in New Salem. They taught me about some of the jobs the people would have done. I got to take pictures with them.

These living history interpreters taught me how to dye yarn.

"Whatever you are, be a good one."
This is one of Lincoln's favorite sayings.
He is often given credit for coining the
phrase, which is also attributed to
William Thackery.

This actor portrays Abraham Lincoln as a surveyor in the movie "In the Declaration all men are created equal:" *Abraham Lincoln in Illinois, 1830 to 1860*, produced by the Witnessing History Education Foundation, Inc's Pageant of America Documentary Series.

While Lincoln lived at New Salem, he had many different jobs. He owned a grocery store. He liked talking with people when they came to the store. He was also the postmaster. He dutifully cared for people's mail. Another job he had was as a surveyor. He measured land to be sure people knew what they owned
and what they did not own.

Lincoln often chopped wood for other families. I was really surprised to learn that Abraham was famous in New Salem for his wrestling skills. I wonder how many presidents could claim great wrestling skills?

Townsfolk prepare for a wrestling match at New Salem.

I was excited to learn that Abraham Lincoln loved animals. However, I am sad to say that Abraham's favorite animals were CATS!
I know! This information is hard to believe. Mrs. Lincoln used to say that cats were Abraham's hobby. When he lived in New Salem, he had two cats named Jane and Susan.

President Lincoln loved his cats so much he let them eat at the dinner table!

Before Lincoln became president, the family had a dog named Fido.

Abraham Lincoln was a loving father. He believed the old saying: "Boys will be boys."
Willie and Tad had permission to interrupt meetings when he was president.

This picture, taken at the Lincoln Presidential Museum, shows patient father Abraham Lincoln relaxing and reading while his son plays.

Learning about the Lincoln family was interesting. Abraham Lincoln and his wife Mary had four sons. Their names were Robert, Edward, William, and Thomas.

Living history interpreters portray Mrs. Lincoln, Willie, and Tad.

The boys had nicknames. Robert was called Bobby, Edward was Eddie, William was Willie, and Thomas was called Tad. Abraham even had a nickname for Mrs. Lincoln—MOLLY! How cool is that?

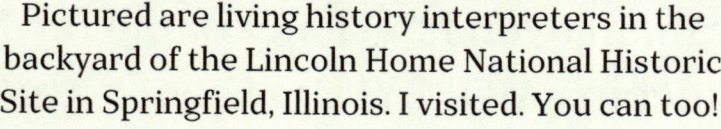

Pictured are living history interpreters in the backyard of the Lincoln Home National Historic Site in Springfield, Illinois. I visited. You can too!

Many people have nicknames. I do. Sometimes I get called Nosey Rosey. Do you have a nickname? There is a funny story about how Tad got his nickname.

When Tad was born, he had a big head and a skinny body. His father looked at him and decided he looked like a tadpole. So, he called him Tad. A tadpole is a baby frog. I am not sure I would want to be named for a frog!!!

Do you see the resemblance?

Tad Lincoln

tadpole

People were supposed to say, "Hello Mr. Lincoln," or, "Hello Abraham." They were NOT supposed to say, "Hey ABE!"

I learned lots of interesting facts about Abraham Lincoln. One thing many people do not know is that he did NOT like to be called ABE. I have even heard people call him "Honest Abe." He would not have liked that, either.

"ABE" is not okay.

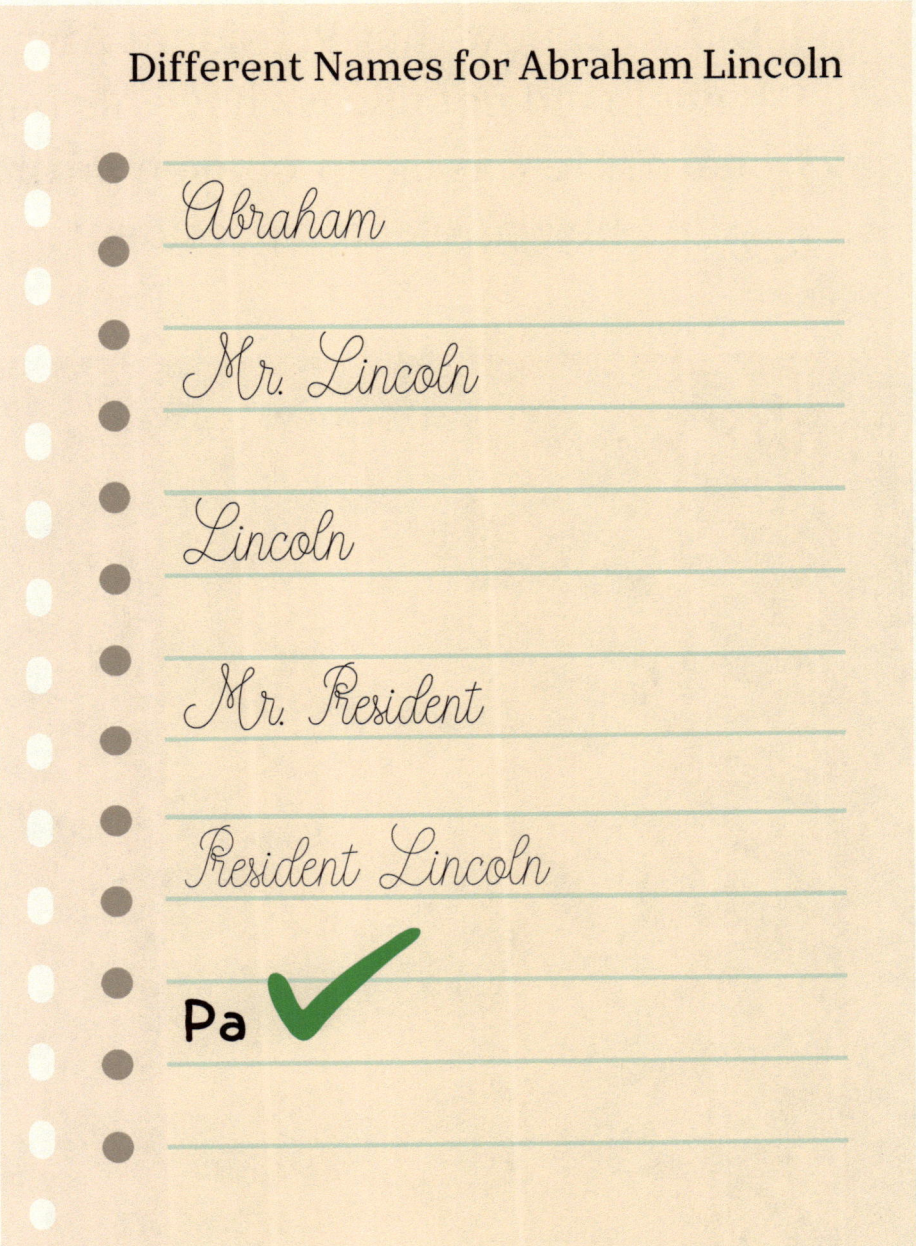

These are the names President Lincoln liked to be called. He wanted people to use Abraham, Mr. Lincoln, or just Lincoln. His sons called him Pa. When he became president, people called him Mr. President.

Did you know that President Abraham Lincoln did not always have his famous beard? He was clean-shaven until after he was elected president.

One day he got a letter from a little girl. Her name was Grace Bedell. She told him that she thought he would look much better with a beard. He must have believed her because he grew his beard. What do you think? Does he look better with or without the beard?

President Lincoln met Grace after she wrote to him! Maybe he wanted to show her his new beard.

President Lincoln had to send
Tad some sad news in a letter to Mrs. Lincoln.

"Tell dear Tad, poor 'Nanny Goat' is lost.
The day you left, Nanny was found
resting herself and chewing her little cud
on the middle of Tad's bed.
But now she's gone!"

When the Lincoln family lived in the White House, Lincoln's sons Willie and Tad had two goats. They were named Nanny and Nanko.

One time the boys hitched the goats to a chair and used the chair as a wagon. Nanny and Nanko trotted Willie and Tad right into a fancy party! They did not even get in trouble. In fact, President Lincoln thought the stunt was funny. I wonder if the goats tried to eat the ladies' pretty dresses?

"The Doll Jack is pardoned, by order of the president." A. Lincoln

I almost forgot to tell you about one of my favorite stories! When the Lincoln family lived in the White House, Willie and Tad liked to dress up and pretend to be soldiers. Their soldier doll named Jack was not a very good soldier because he fell asleep on guard duty. That is terrible behavior for a soldier! He was in big trouble.

Willie and Tad went to their Pa and asked for a pardon for Jack. Since their Pa was president, he was able to formally forgive Jack and save him from being punished.

Pictured are of living history interpreters portraying Willie and Tad at the Lincoln Home National Historic Site.

Did you count as you read my book? Did you learn 10 facts about Abraham Lincoln?

You should have learned:
1. Abraham Lincoln was born February 12, 1809.
2. Lincoln grew up on farm.
3. He lived at New Salem.
4. He liked animals, especially cats.
5. There were six members of the Lincoln family.
6. Family members had nicknames.
7. Lincoln did not like to be called Abe.
8. President Lincoln grew a beard after a young girl wrote him a letter.
9. Willie and Tad had goats at the White House.
10. Willie and Tad requested a presidential pardon for their doll Jack.

Which story was your favorite? Did you learn anything new about Abraham Lincoln that you didn't know before? I hope so!

Love, Molly

Photo resources:
Page 1 by Marla Judge Abraham Lincoln Presidential Museum (ALPM)
Page 5 by Marla Judge
Page 6 artwork by Charmaine Zoe Troup, permission granted
Page 10 National Park Service
Page 11 by Marla Judge at NPS site
Page 12 by Marla Judge at ALPM
Page 13 by Marla Judge at Lincoln's New Salem State Historic Site
Page 14 by Marla Judge
Page 15 by Marla Judge at New Salem
Page 16 by Marla Judge at New Salem
Page 18 taken while filming "In the Declaration all men are created equal:" *Abraham Lincoln in Illinois, 1830 to 1860*
Page 19 by Marla Judge at New Salem
Page 20 public domain
Page 20 public domain
Page 22 by Marla Judge at ALPM
Page 23 by Marla Judge, with permission, taken at Lincoln Home National Historic Site (the boys pictured are Marla Judge's grandsons)
Page 24 by Marla Judge with permission
Page 26 Library of Congress (Tad Lincoln)
Page 26 public domain (tadpole)
Page 30 Library of Congress
Page 31 Library of Congress
Page 32 by Marla Judge
Page 33 public domain
Page 34 Library of Congress
Page 35 by Marla Judge with permission
Page 36 by Marla Judge with permission
Page 42 from supercoloring.com

Photo Locations:
Abraham Lincoln Birthplace National Historical Park
2995 Lincoln Farm Rd, Hodgenville, KY 42748

Lincoln's New Salem State Park
15588 History Lane, Petersburg, IL 62675

Abraham Lincoln Presidential Library & Museum
212 N. 6th St., Springfield, IL 62701

Lincoln Home National Historic Site
413 S. 8th St, Springfield, IL 62701

Living History Interpreters:
Pam Brown as Mary Lincoln, *www.livingmarylincoln.com*
Richard (Fritz) Klein as Abraham Lincoln, *www.lincolninstitute.com*
William Golladay as Willie Lincoln
Samuel Golladay as Tad Lincoln
Robert Judge, Marla Harms Judge, Beth Adams Staff, Paul Golladay, and Peter Hoehnle

Lincoln sites to visit:
*Abraham Lincoln Birthplace National Historic Park
2995 Lincoln Farm Rd, Hodgenville, KY
*Lincoln Boyhood National Memorial
3027 E S St, Lincoln City, In 47552
*Lincoln Monument Association (Lincoln Tomb)
1500 Monument Ave, Springfield, Il 62702
*Lincoln Home National Historic Site
413 S. 8th St, Springfield, Il. 62701
*Abraham Lincoln Presidential Library & Museum
212 N. 6th St., Springfield, IL 62701
*Lincoln Memorial
2 Lincoln Memorial Cir NW, Washington, DC 20002

About the Authors

Molly is a beautiful dalmatian dog. She lives with her human family in a big old house where she is very spoiled!

Marla Harms Judge lives with her husband Robert and Molly. She is a self-proclaimed history geek and book lover. Marla has worked as a school librarian, a park ranger and a living history interpreter. Creating this book (with Molly) brings together all of these interests. Molly and Marla have more books planned, so be sure to stay in touch!

Please write to us at: Mollythehistorydog@gmail.com
Visit: mollythehistorydog.com

Also by Marla Harms Judge:

We send a special thank you to Robert for all his love and support!

Color your own dalmatian puppy!